THE BOY UNDER THE BED

JOHNS HOPKINS: POETRY AND FICTION
John T. Irwin, general editor

Guy Davenport, *DaVinci's Bicycle: Ten Stories*
John Hollander, *"Blue Wine" and Other Poems*
Robert Pack, *Waking to My Name: New and Selected Poems*
Stephen Dixon, *Fourteen Stories*
Philip Dacey, *The Boy under the Bed*

PHILIP DACEY

The Boy under the Bed

The Johns Hopkins University Press
Baltimore and London

This book has been brought to publication with the generous assistance of the G. Harry Pouder Fund.

Library of Congress Cataloging in Publication Data
Dacey, Philip.
  The boy under the bed.
  (Johns Hopkins: poetry and fiction)
  I. Title. II. Series: Johns Hopkins, poetry and fiction.
PS3554.A23B6   811'.54   80-8858
ISBN 0-8018-2601-2   ISBN 0-8018-2602-0 (pbk.)

"Getting Caught in a Rainstorm" is reprinted from *The Massachusetts Review,* © 1978 by The Massachusetts Review, Inc.
  "Where We Were," © 1977 by *Partisan Review.*
  "Mystery Baseball" and "The Sleep" are reprinted from *Prairie Schooner,* © by the University of Nebraska Press.
  "The Bar-Girl" first appeared in *Three Rivers Poetry Journal,* © 1978 by Three Rivers Press.
  Other poems appeared in: *Agni Review, Ardis Anthology of New American Poetry, Ascent, Brother Songs: A Male Anthology of Poetry* (Holy Cow! Press), *Carleton Miscellany, Centennial Review, Chowder Review, Dacotah Territory, Epoch, Georgia Review* ("The Adulterers' Letters," "He Writes an Old Girlfriend and Asks Her to Have an Affair with Him," "Letter: A Family Man Explains His Adultery"), *GiltEdge: New Series, Great River Review* ("Rural Fantasia," "Caroline Naked: A Husband to His Wife," "The Progress of Love"), *Greenfield Review, Greensboro Review, Hampden-Sydney Poetry Review, Hudson Review* ("The Runner"), *Men at Table* (Chowder Chapbooks), *Mississippi Valley Review, The Nation, New Salt Creek Reader, Northeast* ("This Place"), *Ohio Review* ("Permissions"), *Par Rapport, Pebble, Poet and Critic, Poetry* ("From the Clearing," "Praiseful Mouths"), *Poetry Northwest, Poetry Now, Poets of Southwestern Minnesota* (Southwest Minnesota Arts and Humanities Council), *Pushcart Prize II: The Best of the Small Presses, Quarterly West, Remington Review, Sam Houston Literary Review, Shaping: New Poems in Traditional Prosodies* (Dryad), *Southern Poetry Review, Sou'wester, Thought: A Review of Culture and Idea, 25 Minnesota Poets II* (Nodin Press), *Voices.*

for Florence

We must love one another or die.
—W. H. Auden

Tantos días, ay tantos días
viéndote tan firme y tan cerca,
cómo lo pago, con qué pago?
—Pablo Neruda

CONTENTS

I / APPLE-DOORS

THE DOOR PROHIBITED

Do not open this door as part of the morning opening procedure.—Sign on door in library

Let the morning opening procedure begin
but let no one open this door.
This is the door to be opened at night,
if such a door's to be opened at all.
This is the door that can appall
if the light is wrong, or right
for the wrong reasons, this is the door
dependent on the seasons, the door
that changes color, moves
as we move around it, keys
conspicuous in our morning hands.

Let all the other doors be opened now,
the steady ones, the doors that swing on hinges
in and out, the doors we grew up with
and learned to push aside before they came
behind us, obedient in our wake
as we awoke to enter day.
Companion-doors, wife- and husband-
doors, faithful to a fault,
the locks in place and tumbled
to ward off chance, no dice
to catch the weather on the sill.

Let all the doors be opened
but this one. It is a monument
of doors, to doors, and for them. The Door
of Doors. Or the idea of doors, the first
and last, before and after time,

time that is a tick of doors, a rush
of wind let in to chill us
into staying still, a frozen passage
while the door prohibited, the apple-door,
calls, calls nor creaks, a smooth
whistle through a crack, a key-hole

where the eye, placed, sees itself,
the secret, trapped, or simply hiding out.

PERMISSIONS

*In about five minutes you may safely ask the hairs on your
face to grow.*—In a letter from a friend

You may put your hand in the blouse of any woman you know.
You may tell her your secret name.

You have permission to perform extraordinary athletic feats.
You may make the basketball rim close with satisfaction,
    for good,
    after your shot.
You may break the serves of all the heavenly bodies
    attendant at your birth.

When you wake up in the morning, you may go back to bed
    in the lives of other people.
When you go to sleep at night, you may leave on your doorstep
    what you once had permission
    to call your soul.
    It will be a note for some delivery man
    saying you will buy everything.

You are allowed to gamble for the highest stakes.
    If you're in danger of losing your wife, or your children,
    or the idea of yourself you carry like a charm,
    you may pull out of your sleeve
      the card with nothing on it,
      full of possibilities
      like an actor's face.

Should a man on the street or your closest friend
    give you nothing,
    you may take it, and more.

And before the mirror, when you suddenly notice
   lines are forming in your skin,
   remember they are not
   what they seem.
   Rather, an incredibly baroque signature
   is appearing all over your body.
   When you read the name, you have permission to give praise.

MYSTERY BASEBALL

No one knows the man who throws out the season's first ball.
  His face has never appeared in the newspapers,
    except in crowd scenes, blurred.
  Asked his name, he mumbles something
    about loneliness,
    about the beginnings of hard times.

Each team fields an extra, tenth man.
  This is the invisible player,
    assigned to no particular position.
  Runners edging off base feel a tap on their shoulders,
    turn, see no one.
  Or a batter, the count against him, will hear whispered
    in his ear vague, dark
    rumors of his wife, and go down.

Vendors move through the stands
  selling unmarked sacks,
  never disclosing their contents,
  never having been told.
  People buy, hoping.

Pitchers stay busy
  getting signs.
  They are everywhere.

One man rounds third base, pumping hard,
  and is never seen again.
  Teammates and relatives wait years at the plate,
    uneasy, fearful.

An outfielder goes for a ball on the warning track.
  He leaps into the air and keeps rising,
    beyond himself, past
    the limp flag.
  Days later he is discovered,
    descended, wandering dazed
    in centerfield.

Deep under second base lives an old man,
  bearded, said to be
  a hundred. All through the game,
  players pull at the bills of their caps,
  acknowledging him.

THE ORGY

We were invited
but we didn't go.
We thanked them kindly,
then said no.

Too many knees,
we said. An eye
could get put out
that way.

We'd seen pictures;
we'd read books.
Better stay home
in certain nooks.

At orgies things
don't stay in place:
a heap of flesh
becomes a living face.

A hand from nowhere
reaches out
and won't let go
of what it's got

and what it's got
is you, you, you;
giving in is what
you have to do.

The room's a heaving
flood of parts,
breasts, bellies,
elbows, hearts:

thus would we all
disintegrate;
and there's a rule
to follow: mate.

The god of orgies
is Disorder,
who loves to trample
on a border.

What would we do
without the line
that runs between
your piece and mine?

An orgy has a clear
and simple cost:
the will to chance
the getting lost.

The invitation said,
R.S.V.P.
We did, but,
strange to see,

we wept as we declined.
And stranger still:
another invitation
soon came in the mail.

EMPTYING YOUR POCKETS

It takes years.
You never knew
you had so many pockets,
that you had collected
so much.
        In one
your parents click together,
cool marbles you roll
off your thumb into the circle;
you lose them
to a sharpie.
Your first love
has a pocket all to herself:
as trim as a knifeblade,
she slides along your finger
as she always did,
getting in
but not far enough.
In another are your wife
and children:
that pocket is sewn up
and the threads
have vanished
as after a successful
operation.
The pocket for the other
woman
is unobtrusive,
lies flat against your thigh,
but you know she is there
and know you need
do nothing about it:

that pocket always
empties itself.
In another your friends
are concerned for you,
like important reminders
jotted down in a rush;
you can't read them;
you throw them away, wondering
what they are saying.
Everything you wanted to do
but were afraid of
fills several pockets:
these are the hardest to empty
since there is nothing there.
When you come to the last pocket
you discover it is full
of empty pockets.
This is the only one
you tell yourself
you must never empty.

FROM THE CLEARING

Of course, the forest that was here, a condition
    To wander in, is now there, a circle
Keeping its distance, and the flowers in the open
    Outperform those in the deep well
Of the woods, but the beautiful animals,
    Whose coming led me to this eye of day,
Have gone. If I had known then, when I saw
    The last hoof flash in the clearing like a signal
And the underbrush shake to receive the body
    Of the leaping animal, that what befell
The forest was not only an absence but a final
    Absence, that it indeed *was* the last hoof,
I would not have considered myself so safe
    From some general dark will; that is to say,
From the forest itself. For it had been the very
    Appearance of the animals that originally
Threw back, or seemed to throw back,
    The shadows onto themselves. And that
Was because the darkness the animals brought
    With them was deeper, richer, was black.

Then it was a case of one darkness against another,
    But now it is a case of this light against
The animals themselves—the light I was happy
    To see enter me when I entered it—or, rather,
This light in *place* of the animals. For they
    Cannot abide it, and will not lie down
With it. Although this seemingly constant noon—
    What shadows there are are touchingly small—
Is itself beautiful, I cannot help but wonder
    Which to prefer: life in the clearing
Without animals, or life in the forest

With them. Could I have been wrong
To follow them this far? Or was it the staying
   Here so long that got me talking
To myself? The irony is obvious:
   They brought me out whom I betray
By my readi—no, by my willingness
   To see night wait on day.

     O Nameless Beasts now gone,
       I pray you lie somewhere in wait—
     If not in this too bright light
       Nor in the deep glades you are kin
     To but oppose, then in some border
       Land men cross going from here
     To there, with them the gods of transition—
       And do not disdain to help again
     One you helped before. I know
       I tell of fixity, the sun halt
     In a blue sky, no lengthening shadow
       Across a leisurely expanse of green,
     But hear me—for amusement, for love—
       When I say I dreamed a circle shut,
     I dreamed the very woods began to move.

RURAL FANTASIA

The schoolbus drivers enter their buses
at seven o'clock in the morning.
They enter their buses to pick up
the children, who have waited all night,
alone, at the ends of driveways,
their little lunches tight in their hands.
Someone would be touched to see them,
their still, patient bodies marking
the prairie landscape under moonlight,
under morning sun, but no one sees them.
Not the parents, who dream in their neat
farmhouses that the children are their own,
like shocks of wheat, nor the bus drivers,
who, in the far town, can only imagine
the children and think of them as pilots
on a dawn airstrip, the crucial mission
assigned to their squadron, would think of
islands, the future's beautiful atolls.
Meanwhile the children wait. What else is there
to do at the roadside, dressed in good clothes,
as the stars turn away, ashamed again?
At eight o'clock, the children will enter
the buses, will know the jounce, the sway,
will be carried down the road, waving
at cars behind them. At eight o'clock,
the heart of one driver will break to think
of the children, the parents, the stars, and
himself, will flood with tears like a fuel
the lines and chambers of the bus and propel
it, dream-quick, to a place before one child.
The door will breathe open and a small foot
will lift toward the first step, at eight.

Which will never come. It is seven o'clock.
It is always seven o'clock in the morning.
The drivers enter their buses, then enter
again, perfect at beginning, as if
beginning were best, and bore repeating.
The stars knew all along the buses would
never pick up the children. The stars knew
how it almost happened, or happens, or will,
that the distance between drivers and children
is only this much, a key will enter it,
nothing else, the thinnest key to ignite
fire, thin enough to see through.
They are that close, prairie and town
collapse to an eye, an eye seeing
itself or another, all the air
between as yellow with sun as a bus.

II / SPANISH ARTIFACTS

WATCHING A MOVIE IN A FOREIGN LANGUAGE
WITHOUT SUBTITLES (Cordoba)

This is the way it has always been:
Someone speaks, and you know
You will never understand.
A man shoots another man
And talks as he does.
You try to translate. Could he have said,
"We are all dying loaves of bread"?
Or a woman opens her blouse,
Revealing a scar on her breast.
To the man who stares, you hear her say,
"Yes, yes, there are rivers in the moon. Jelly."
For years now, you have starred
In your own foreign movie.
Once, at breakfast,
When the sun through the terrace window
Was a director's dream,
Your wife said, "You know, I love you."
It was the strangest language you had ever heard;
You passed her the salt.
Or your children run to the door to greet you,
Chanting, "Daddy's home! Daddy's home!"
Your eyes fill with tears,
Surely out of frustration:
When will they learn to speak
The tongue of men?
So you eat popcorn, heavily buttered,
And watch the inexplicable goings-on:
A car hurtles off a cliff;

The sun rises.
Leaving the theatre, someone bumps into you.
He says, "Savages have eaten the moon."
You say, "You're welcome,"
And smile. It is always good
To meet someone from home.

JANUARY 1, 1974 (Altea)

It was a thin bough from our Christmas tree
(The tree that wasn't one, actually,
But a poor tossed-away remnant from a pine
Florence salvaged from the dump in town
And decorated, Emmett helping out,
With ornaments they made by hand and wit)
That I broke off and strung, a fishing rod,
For Austin, because he'd cried, who went and stood
Before the fire lighting up that room
And held that rod, like so, and fished for flame.

WAKING SLOWLY AFTER A SIESTA (Altea)

The world comes slowly back
As if it means to make
Me notice it was gone
And now is here again,
Or not exactly here
But forming in the air.
It's such a lovely state,
This coming back, this not
Yet being where the world
Before had me ensnarled
But being on the way,
I sleepily try to woo
It into holding still,
Like something I could will.
This world comes slowly back
And seems a happy trick:
It comes without its weight
That falls so like a boot;
Its edges, sharp before,
Appear all softened.
                      Here
My body knows all's right
And feels like a sailboat
On a balmy day at sea:
It navigates with so
Easy a way between
The worlds of water and sun,
Between sleep and the light,
A perfect form for spirit,

I think I must excuse
Its feeling as it does
That it's possessed of all
The grace it needs or will
Need ever for its sake.
Slowly, the world comes back.

THE BAR-GIRL (Alicante)

aimless sexual energy—Lawrence Ferlinghetti

I toss an orange into the air
and catch it, because no one's here
to wait on. This life is a bore,
and so I look at you there
with your nose in a cold beer
and at him with the newspaper
and out the window where the roar
of motorcycles is adventure,
but I've seen it all before
and so I take another
orange, and then one more
and feel how heavy they are
and look at their bright color
and grace the rough sphere
of each with a finger.
What am I waiting for?
If someone comes in the door
or not, I don't care.
And I don't care either
if an orange should disappear
when I toss it into the air.

PRISMS (Altea)

It was a rainbow impossibly
beautiful, straddling the town
with one foot poised lightly on the sea

and the other set atop the mountain
behind us. It was a fairy-tale
rainbow if there ever was one.

For days rain had made a jail
of the world, but now Emmett and I
were out walking; when we stopped to marvel

at the banded color and he asked, Why
are there rainbows? I explained how water,
a prism, builds archways in the sky.

Days later, as we sat together
in the plaza, each with paper and pen
to write or draw, Emmett's clear

plastic ballpoint bent the sun-
light into a rainbow on his wrist.
We both laughed: it was small and thin

but there it was. Who could have guessed
prisms wait in disguise right under
our noses, that when you least

expect it a prism will appear,
breaking the light to show its color?

GETTING CAUGHT IN A RAINSTORM (Altea)

I can't say it was exactly fun,
The way the rain
Beat on my head and drowned my eyes
To make a haze
Of where I went, so that I saw
Only a sea
Of vague figures, nothing true,
Or how I'd try,
By lowering my head, to get
My footsteps right
Between the rivers forming on
The street's incline,
The world's essence incarnate come
To wash me home
(Although the getting dry was good,
With the fire red
And leaping in the darkened room,
The rising steam
From lemonade laced with whiskey,
And the fine bouquet
Of your hair across my shoulder),
But if ever
The chance came to do it again,
If the sky ran
Over with rain like a blessed cup
From which a sip
Meant the whole engulfing thing,
If all along
My world's margins bad weather set
Its clear limit,
Speaking in unmistakable tones
To my poor bones'

Marrow about cold, and if it were
A choosing matter,
I think I'd still choose getting soaked,
Because I liked
The weather's honesty with me—
How it dashed my
Face with what it had to say,
"Inclemency,"
Leaving to Man any disguise—
But more because
I liked the way the water brought
The colors out.

III / NIPPLES RISE TO SPIRIT

THE BOY UNDER THE BED

The boy under the bed
hears his parents,
who do not hear him
breathing so carefully.
They are declaring their presence
above him,
like gods,
with their own rhythms,
their own seasons,
and the voices
blur into clouds,
peaks he saw in a book
of gods his mother's fingers
walked through as if
she owned where the gods lived.
This is thunder,
he thinks,
and I am rain.
Or lightning.
Or only the underside
of thunder.

Later he will say
there was water,
which he was,
and they were the boat,
or he was

and they were waves
one wave
suspended above him,
a frozen heaven of death
holding off
till he told them good night.

SLEEPING PARENTS, WAKEFUL CHILDREN

When our parents were sleeping
We brought them gifts
It was a whispering time
The great bodies lain down
Upon the long bed
The deep sighs adrift
Through the upper rooms
It was a whispering time
When the gods slept
And we made gifts for them
With paints paper and tiny
Scissors safe for us
Masks and rings
Obscure magical things
In the halted hour
In the still afternoon
The anger asleep
And the jokes we didn't understand
The violent love
That carried our weather
All subsided to these
Two vulnerable ones
Their hands and mouths
Open like babes'
Their heads high
In the pillowy clouds
For all we knew dreaming us
Sneaking in
Lest they woke and discovered
Our love our fear
How we thrilled to appease
Praise and thank

Them in secret
My sister and I
Approaching the border
The edge of the platform
Where the gods murmured
So precise in our placement
Of these our constructions
Frivolous fair
The gifts on the skirts
Of their lives for surprise
Then turning away
Lips and fingers a cross
When they opened their eyes
They would never know how
When or why
They would never know
Who we were

THREE FOR THE FATHER

1. The Coal Furnace

It was down my father went
to the basement
where he shoveled
in the coal.

The winter night
and red yellow
and leaping the fire
my father was keeping.

There was deep chill
somewhere in the house
beyond the fire,
the marriage broke,

but there were nights
my father went into
the slatted coalbin
(in fall, the rattle

down the chute, and once
childish sex there)
and in the coalbin
scraped the scrape of need—

shovel on cement,
through coaldust,
the metal rasp
to pick the nuggets up.

I'd swing open the furnace door
and he'd fling in
the black and shining
sacrifice against the cold.

More shovelsful, with care
to bank the coal just right,
and always at the end:
"There, that will last the night."

2. His Father Takes Up Gardening Late in Life

What do you do among the tomato plants?
Tell me the same stories
you tell the roots and vines.

Here, after so long, you've learned to bury
each mistake, then take it weeks later
between your thumb and finger and break it off.

I am there, helmeted in green leaves,
and grow new,
a perfect specimen.
You eat your child clean
this time, and I am done,
but in my own heaven.

How did you know your memory
lay like good dirt in a backyard,
and would yield old faces,
words, deeds, each morning
like a cymbal crash,
only now leafed and in color,
made over like a new start?

Greet me as you greet them,
with your fingers framing a marvelous tale
of a short, happy life,
and I shall be all seed
and set myself
at many tables.

3. First Snow

My father in the snow
before the window
where he called to me
to see what fell,
was falling, and would fall.
My father lower
than the level of the sill
and looking up, his face
lit by what flooded past
the drapes I pushed aside
in answer to his call.
My father gone outside
perhaps to walk, to practice
walking for a later time
he'd walk away for good,
but turned back now to be
a face remembering me,
the child of the snow,
calling me to see my parents
falling through the night,
more parents than I could count
and each unique
and meant to catch upon the tongue
though glass prevented that
and I could only watch
the long descent
and watch his face get all the light,
as if at center stage,
or all except what spilled

around his shoes
or lit the faces of the snow,
the faces easy in the wind
but blank to eyes
as young as mine,
and I the master
of that stage because
I held the curtain back
and, seeing, let it fall,
not thinking to applaud
the show but turning full
away
to something I no longer know.

THE MERMAID CRASHED UPON THE MIND

The mermaid crashed upon the mind
of the young man, took it
by surprise, and near broke it
before he surfaced to his kind.

Down below he had turned with her,
twisted and whorled the water so
his mind had gone out to the green glow
of that world; he had loved that water.

Don't imagine it would be any different
with yourself; her hands were loose
and firm all at once, he said yes
to whatever way she went,

and thought her hair was the hair
of his mother, who he thought was dead:
it trailed away like a wet road
promising this way was as good as air.

And her skin, it locked in
secrets and showed them, too:
her body was a window
and not to look was the sin.

Love under water! He was young
and the dry air was dry.
What did he care for the sun's eye
or that he'd lose his tongue?

He wanted a sense of water, over
and under him. And her thoughtless hips
accompanied him like fine music, the tips
of her breasts said ever, ever.

A mermaid crashed upon the mind
of a young boy, wrapped her tail
between his legs and played till
bored, then forced him to ascend.

Now he, gone mute, can only walk
all day around our dusty town—
except for pausing to pretend to swim
under the bank's clock.

IN HER EAR

By tone and rhythm, by poetic and musical qualities
words became a special bond between . . . lovers who
needed an extra outlet for their enchantment
and ecstasy.—Lewis Mumford

They needn't be words the dictionary
knows. They needn't be words at all. They needn't
be more than a cast of a line, a bond
between you and her, for as long as they sound.
What bonds is something in the ear, you place
it there and move it in and out, it gets
itself with other sounds and grows big, big
enough to fill the cavity the head
has cocked for evidence of love it lost
long ago in a silence of bodies.
The thing in the ear is decoration,
scrollwork all around her head, close-fitting
exuberance that twists and turns to keep
a ball in motion, a trick animals
dream of in their cages, the savannah
stretching like a bed green with its promise.
The ear listens, widens and shrinks, widens
again only to shrink around a note
tight enough to hold it in and test it
along the ways of gates, canals, the ear
connects to and she inhabits as waves
inhabit water, or water waves. Say
Waves to her. Waves of feeling. Make waves
together. Ride them out, like a storm. Like
a wind whipped to a frenzy for the sake
of a good story, and you can tell it:
once upon a time. And then it gets blue.
The blue sounds bend like dream-girders for a

round house, a dome to call your own the earth
matches, sighing. In this sigh, syllables
bubble, percolate to the edge of words
and back again then up up and over.
The body translates to language and language
to body. Which came first? Let's go round
this way without an answer, a uroboros
eating its own tail, fattening on its
long dying. Her ear is a grave gone
cornucopian; lay the bodies down
then prepare to catch the yield in your arms.
Love loves an alphabet, a trip on the tip
of a tongue, a flower of air budding
on the stem of a throat. Graduate
to a bouquet. Give it to her. You'll find yourself
thick in petals, thumbing a children's book
of adult knowledge, the first page and last,
the beginning and end, torn out in a
passion of labials and gutterals,
a bright body yawning between two darks.

CAROLINE NAKED: A Husband to His Wife

She was naked there, your little sister
(Not so little, sixteen, big enough),
In our bedroom, where she'd gone to change out
Of her bathing suit. I thought she was still
Down at the pool, so I walked in without
Knocking, Actaeon to her Artemis.
She was white where her two-piece suit failed
To let the sun in, and brown everywhere else.
By the clock, it was no more than a second
We stood there, exchanging surprised looks,
But the second, for me, isn't over yet:
It was a moment outside of time, and so
Was not a moment but a gap through which
Things came rushing, all at once, a skein of light
And dark things I am still unraveling.
What rushed in, one strand of light or dark, I
Don't know which, was you, Wife. It was not
Your body, yet it was. You were there, behind
The flesh and form, as if you'd put it all on
Like a new dress, as if you and your sister
Were one woman and every woman's body
In the world were but a vestment for her.
And lust, of course, came through the gap in time,
But lust, because of shock, transformed. Surely
The hunter, when he saw Diana, greed-
lessly loved the form so suddenly revealed
In the woods' clearing—it had the shock of art,
But wasn't art at all, though out of time
And purified.
                    The dogs, too, came rushing through.
My dogs, trained to seize my prey, seized me,
Stag, and the hunter was got. I was torn

Apart, for my own sake, by my fierce teeth:
I mean, Wife, your sister's naked body
Destroyed (destroys in that continuing instant)
My old, poorer self who'd never seen
The other world shining through her flesh,
The world that made wherever your sister
Was standing the room's, my day's center.
And I, without thought, but with the will
Of my body, concurred, self-devourer.
And other things (besides the simple sight
Of breasts, belly, the dark triangle, all
The parts, and the whole they serve) swarmed me: rich
Silences, possibilities like shapely
Fire-goddesses, and forces naked
But for the nakedness they wore as robe.
In short, there was a body, matter, and more.
I opened the door, and looked, and shut it.

Afterwards I saw your sister downstairs
Reading a magazine as she sipped a Coke
And waiting, in a party dress, for her date.
Our eyes met again, but now within the frame
Of time, and so I thought her eyes said this:
"I deny it all; it's a pretty lie.
I am no fire-goddess; I chew gum.
If I am sexy, what is that? A pout,
A glance from heavily made-up eyes. You
Imagine great roots and channels running
From me to wells beyond us. You may thirst,
But this flesh, promiseful and deep to you,
Is made for one lover: dark and faithful
To a fault, he woos with a bouquet of shadows."

Then her date rang the bell and she got up
To go. In my eyes, for her to read, was this:
"I know I am no longer Actaeon,
Nor stag, nor are you surprised Artemis
(Though your dress reveals by the very act
Of hiding); I know this world waits for you,
Handsome in a fashionable sport coat.
Still, there are clearings everywhere, open
Spaces we come upon, or that come upon us,
Unexpectedly: there the familiar
Changes, burns; nipples rise to spirit.
There is no end to the disguises of doors."
Hurrying out, your sister left the door
Ajar. Wife, I went after, to close it.
It swung there, in the breeze, between this and
That. I secured it, then heard you elsewhere
In the house, going from one room to another.

THE KITCHEN: THREE POEMS

1. On Getting a Circular Table

It's about time. The four of us hardly
fit anymore around the odd-shaped
cripple you and I found in a dark corner
of the Salvation Army store at Hope and Cross
Avenues twelve long years ago. Oh
I put in a few nails and steadied it
but God knows its small five-sided top
was meant only to display potted plants or
old photos, not serve a hungry family.
It's gone now, taken to the city dump
on the far side of town where it's at home
with the debris of other families—
broken lamps, boxes with their bottoms out,
all of it sinking beneath weeds and pierced
through by wildflowers.
                              In its place is what,
gnawed by late hunger and come down for a snack,
I have found here in the center of the kitchen
so lit by moonlight through the window
as to seem not entirely of this world,
our table coolly washed by the faintest
blue light, that washes the room, and all set
for breakfast, for anything. Each separate
piece of silverware and china occupies
the place each should occupy. The napkins
lie upon themselves in deep repose.
It is a magic circle, what nowadays we
sit and talk and eat around, each of us
on the rim of the wheel. I think it turns
and we turn with it. I think its speed is

immeasurable, so that we cannot know
if there's a danger we'll be spun off; we
hold on—not from fear, but for
the holding on, and for the holding to
each other. It makes no difference that
now the three of you sleep time away
upstairs while I stand here awake, apart;
we always bend, nor break, to Circle, home,
our faces to the center and ourselves
even though to all appearances we
fall away, centrifugal and back to back.

Now I go for the refrigerator.
The harsh square of light I open up blasts
the room all-instantaneously to
a remembered dream; such light as hunger
throws around on everything outmuscles
the light fine enough to be some kind of
achievement. Now I'm merely a man
with the makings of a sandwich, a top
and bottom, plus the works, like the classic
short story: beginning, muddle, and end.
It's a pile, and leans, but the lure of it
brought me down here, wide-eyed, in the first place.

2. This Place

*Poetry and Hums aren't things which you get,
they're things which get you. And all you can do
is go where they can find you.*—Milne, *The House
at Pooh Corner*

Surely, this must be the wrong place:
There is white bread here, and butter,
And two loud boys on the staircase;
Everything around me is familiar,
As unstrange as their mother's face.

I had expected something different:
A burning valley, let's say, where
Blue horses circle a glass tent,
Or, at least, a high, thin ledge for
A man to totter on, in torment.

But this is where the signs led me,
To a house where the smell of supper
Fills the air and a table is ready
With things as common as water
(Or as rare, to one uncommonly dry).

The woman at the stove fries meat
And potatoes, plain, basic fare—
Something, like a refrain, to repeat.
The song it's from surrounds us here;
We're what it sings, who've come to eat.

3. Hortatory

Let the refrigerator open by itself.
Let the food, if there is food, speak.
Let the light, if there is a light,
if the lightbulb works, shine on the words
the food speaks. Let the food
identify itself—a carton of milk,
a firing squad of eggs,
a ball of cheese brooding
upon the family, if there is a family,
asleep upstairs. Then let the family
awaken, as from a dream,
father, mother, son, and daughter,
each sit up as one,
as from the same bad moment
in the same dream, the dream
of a kitchen where hunger
awakens, where the light,
that shone on the words,
if they were spoken,
is spilled like milk.
And let them all come down,
who were sleeping,
who will sleep again,
and enter the kitchen.
Let them find the milk in the carton,
the eggs whole, the cheese
secure in its rind.
And let the refrigerator
close by itself, if it is open,

if it ever was open,
but not before they eat,
the lover, the loved, the children of love,
the children of appetite, blood of it,
blood and milk, let the kitchen
be innocent, if not clean.

THE LIVING ROOM

*I love to photograph people's living rooms . . .
and mirrors.* —Elsa Dorfman

This is the place where it all happened,
　　Though no one knows precisely what.
Once there was a family here, then there was not.
　　The scattered papers and overturned glass tend
To confirm those who lived here left in a hurry:
　　An open window leads some to suspect
A natural occurrence—a wind, a vortex—
　　Wrapped them up and blew them away;
Other, more level-headed authorities
　　Believe if there was a wind it was one
Inside them, a kind of family wind
　　That harried the blood but left the trees
Thoroughly unmolested. According to that
　　Theory they blew themselves out
Of each other's lives with centrifugal
　　Motion and haven't stopped yet.
Though there were children, it is impossible
　　To determine the exact number,
For the discovery of both a mature
　　Fingerprint on a toy by that end table
And certain words and phrases in a hastily
　　Penned and half-finished letter
Suggests that calendar-age was no guarantee
　　Against the, say, youthfulness of any member.
Pictures of ancestors crowd one wall;
　　Whoever lived here had a sense
Of history, though whether the consequence
　　Of that was an abiding good cheer
Or deep despair is a question still

In need of an answer. Thus it is the mirror
Over the mantelpiece that deserves most
     Careful attention. Stand before it
And you can see behind you the dark ghosts
     Of those whose absence is at issue, yet
Turn around to catch them in your own
     Two eyes and they are gone.
Perhaps they disappear inside you,
     Like divers for treasure, some lost jewel
The family staked its reputation on
     And that now you alone,
Without your knowledge, carry. Or perhaps
     The ghosts themselves are treasure,
What you must redeem from behind glass
     And, at all times, proudly, wear.
But all that is speculation. What is not,
     However, is the richness of this carpet
We stand on. One could get lost
     In its design and easily pretend
The whole masterpiece is Being's ground,
     Despite, or because of, one badly worn spot.

ADULTERY: A TRIPTYCH

1. The Adulterers' Letters

I. To His Mistress from Abroad

It has been raining here a lot, and you
Are there. What the gulls cry is not
Your name, though I have thought so.
There are feminine forms everywhere:
Softly rounded hills plump the horizon
And the sea heaves like a bosom.
My memory shifts and turns, like someone
Trying to go to sleep. Still, if I said
Nothing here holds me, it would not be true.

Even the simple orange, especially the simple orange,
Here becomes a whole, sweet world. I weigh it, slowly
Peel it, then, one section at a time,
Savor it. I dream oranges. Also, remember
When you saw my wife and children from a distance
And said, "They're beautiful," and I said, "Yes, they are,"
And there was silence between us for an hour?
Here, if it isn't the rain washing their faces,
It's the sun drying them; either way, I'm a man
Lost and helpless, with everywhere to turn to.

Except for evil, that dark absence threatening
Always to draw whatever is into it,
The world is all good. And it is great.
I think it is too much to hold at once.
I try, and feel it spill away. We are
Cursed with a lovely abundance.

I choose the beautiful moods of the sea,
And I choose the dizzying peaks, inland.
We are men at table, too hungry to eat well.

II. Her Answer

The world grows smaller every day.
You are abroad, with them, and say
There is too much to choose between.
Would you say that if you had seen
What I have seen, a shadow loom
Long in my mirror? Once there was room
In the world for me and mine, but now
There is this pressing near my brow.
Sometimes I sit and hold my head
Like a lone, threatened treasure; naked
After a bath, I have marked where
Flesh wants to give itself to air,
Fall and diffuse away, and I
Am afraid. You give more body
To my body: that is the meaning
Of all my soft sighs when I cling.

I do not know if you are right
Or I am. Alone late at night
I know I am. But, I confess,
Ripe fruit in the mouth is no less
Sweet to me than it is to you.
But once it is eaten, what do we do?
Fruit has its seasons, in—or out.

And what is my season? Do not doubt
I love you, nor that I wait well,
But know that here, in my world, whole
Days unaccountably disappear
With me in them. Sweet, perhaps there,
Touring the islands or a quaint town,
You'll notice, as the sun goes down,
Your shadow, too. It creeps slowly,
But fast enough. Come back to me.

2. He Writes an Old Girlfriend and Asks Her to Have an Affair with Him

I shall be passing through your city soon.
Do you remember me? I was the one
Who was always honest with you and so
Loved you so badly. If you say you do
Not remember, I shall be grateful. If
You say you do, I shall be pleased. My life
Since I last saw you has gone on and on.
I love my wife and children more than
I can say, and I have thought of your face
And body often. Is it from weakness
I think of you often, or from the strength
I felt when I encompassed all the wealth
Of the world by slipping my arms around your waist?
Mind you, I do not feel poor. I can waste
My life, there is so much of it. Will you
Have some?
                    Soon I shall be passing through
Another mirror into another world.
It seems each day now is a solid mirror
I go through, magically, to reappear
All smiles the next day, on the other side,
Newborn amidst the strange and glittering hoard
The plain present is. If ever I am bored,
I am to blame, and you are, who are not here,
Who are only everywhere, the other
Woman. Always lovely in the minds of men,
You glow vaguely along a horizon,
The light for a sentimental scene in a movie.

Then there is the dream. You have come to me
Over and over in the same dream. I am
A hunter out with his dogs. The dim
Forest is uncommonly still, as if paused
Between two worlds. The air is close until
We enter a clearing and find you poised
Naked by a pool beneath a waterfall.
You do not see us and begin to bathe.
I think even the dogs hold their breath
As water you've cupped and lifted flows
Down your back in the sun.
                                        The moment is
One that lasts forever and is quickly
Over. You turn, as if you could hear me
Not breathing, and see us who have seen you
As we never should and still expect to
Live. You approach, and threaten, but before
You can change me to the stag in the old story,
Or to a dog, or change my dogs to men,
I waken, always, wondering what would happen
If I stayed asleep. I am awake now
And wondering what will happen if I go
Back to sleep. Will you let me go to sleep
In your life?
                    With something like love,
                                        Philip

P.S. I think you should know that each year
I grow a year younger, and I laugh more
Than I used to. I think this letter is funny;
I hope you will take it seriously.

As I write, the leaves are falling from the trees.
It is October, everywhere. The wind blows
Down from the North and there is nothing to do
But love it. So I play the great Fool. Who
Does not?
        I look forward to hearing from you.

3. Letter: A Family Man Explains His Adultery

She is not so beautiful as my wife
but death has lately made me crazy.
A friend by gun, another in a car,
and then my aunt by window nine floors up.
Oh, I can sleep all right but when I do
I dream a woman's face comes close and closer
till we kiss:
        I have never seen her before
but somehow know she is everything that is
and chooses me for lover.
        So I, awake,
choose this other. It is my way of going
back to sleep and furthering the dream.

Or so death makes me think. Death says no
over and over, till I go sentimental
and can't say no at all. Women, who are
the world, walk through the world as lure
for leaning me, still dizzy from a fall.
Sirens call through the night, and sirens call.

The defense rests
        uneasy in its bed.
I do not know how not to be the Fool.
I am the man on a banana peel,
who falls so badly as to be a show,
or he who watches, safe, off to the side,
footsure and smirking, rightsideup and proud.
I do not know who is the bigger fool.
The first loses everything in his arms,
and it is small comfort to say man has

nothing, never did, and loss is but a
coming home to oneself, or one's notself.
But the other, all the packages tucked
neatly to his side, does not go down to
taste, nor eat, nor yet learn to live on
the fare of dust and dirt under his shoes.
And then there is the fool who breaks silence.

I break silence again to say God knows
how it will all end. I'd like to think my aunt
and two friends have become guardian angels
and that six dark wings surround me
as I go between the two women.
                                       Anyway I hear
something blowing, a wind, even
in the stillest time.
                       I'd like to think
I love someone, or some two, and all
my children.
                I'd like to think.

Instead I kiss,
           even this,
                  I bend
to paper as to water by a shore
then bend a little more
                    like one who, caught
by a face below, leans far enough to drown.

STUDY

I

There is, perhaps, nothing to say:
Only that a woman, naked
And holding an orange, lies in bed.
It is a scene painters portray.

II

But no, already, see, she moves.
Slowly, she peels the orange until
The fruit is naked as well. Still,
Who can say what the gesture proves?

III

But further now: she eats, one section
At a time. Time is what she seems
To have—and sweet juice. Say, then, dreams
Alone shock us with more perfection.

IV

That said, confess it inadequate:
See how, because she stretches so,
Her full breasts lift as if to show
Words best leave flesh inviolate.

THREE ANNIVERSARIES

1

Five years.
The wooden anniversary.
We like wood, believe it's
trustworthy.

Trees take you, all
kinds: manrockets goal-
bound or low
green clouds, pure sleep.

And wooden sculpture,
for us, has roots,
is still wet
with under-earth.

Our house will be wood.
We'll grow into it
like living wood ourselves,
branching out with children,

and it will grow
into us, turning us
supple but strong
in storms.

I say this: each anniversary
of our wedding
will amaze us
with its rich smell of wood.

2. The Progress of Love

It's been ten years since first your body
Fell out of the sky into my hands.
You were for me such a simple rain
And I caught you so thoughtlessly. Love,
Then all the colors of our touching
Were primary, and green was our bed.

The weather that came into that bed
Wildly spun the vane of the body
And blew us through landscapes of touching.
It was rich soil we held in our hands,
Though we thought merely to dream of love
Would make it leaf out, rain or no rain.

Such dreaming brought us a storm of rain.
We stood in it and stood it. The bed
We slept in held the shape of our love
Rough hewn by inclemency. Body
To body, we studied with our hands
The ways of gentling wind by touching,

The wind that mixed the colors. Touching
Each other, we learned to make a rain
That washed clean the world between our hands,
Though all the while something shook our bed.
On the trembling ground of the body,
We surveyed to build a house of love.

Such innocence! We didn't know love
Turns into snow. O, it was touching,
What we didn't know. So your body
Taught my body and mine yours how rain,
Transformed all beautifully, fills bed
After bed with toys for empty hands.

And when we began to spread our hands
Skyward and wait for the falling love,
Our own sea-change took place in that bed:
We saw how a cold shadow touching
All things deepened them beyond mere rain;
We marked the seasons of the body.

Now there's nothing our hands aren't touching:
We've come to love what happens to rain.
I turn in bed and graze your body.

3

Twelve years,
the silk anniversary.
Things have not been that smooth,
though they have taken

the light in an interesting way
and given it back
so that we call them
shining things.

Silk is cool. We
are not, have never been,
though if we touched
our years they would seem fruit:

I think an apple has silk skin.
I would dress you in silk.
Then undress you.
The clothes would flow off your back

like water, like
slippery time,
that silk tick
between our fingers.

Twelve years!
Would you believe it?
Would you believe a worm
in search of a cocoon

could make such a thing
as all this
we have been wrapped up in
for so long?

Bolts of cloth
as good as breath
spill
all colored and prodigal.

BEDTIME SONG

To sleep in the house of children,
In the house that children sleep in,
Is to sleep in the arms of children's
Dreams, that are dreaming the house,
And to dream you are the children
That are sleeping themselves into dream.

And to sleep in that house is to sleep
In the children, who are the house,
Who are the dark you sleep in
And the arms that hold you asleep,
And to dream in that dark is to house
The children, and you, for the night.

To sleep in a house that dreams
Children is to sleep well, to arm
Yourself for the night is to sleep
In the childish dark, and to dream
Of waking is to waken the child
Who is yourself, dreaming

Of sleep in the children's house.

THE DRINKING

I waken,
middle of the night,
and find your side of the bed
cold,
the sheets thrown back.

And I hear in the next room
Austin gulping your milk.
A great silence in the house
and he at the center,
gulping.

In the dark of his room,
your breast must seem
something not separate
from the darkness,
a vague place
where the dark has brightened.

Drowsy,
I fight sleep
to listen to him drink
as long as I can.

A WIFE

The children hang on me.
Awake, asleep,
they hang on me.
They are bright fruit
on a tree.
They load,
and bless,
me in a time
of ripeness.
But I recall a thin
sapling, just there enough
to bear itself.
Then it was touch
and go, all a fine
uncertainty.
Now what it's become
no wind can shake.
It's there to stay.
You needn't ask,
if you've need,
Where is it today?
I am the tree
and I am tired
of reliability.
    Just once
I would move,
would take a step
this way, or that,
magical,
a root up-pulled
and tentative in the air,
trembling toward a place.

Perhaps in setting down
I'd jostle something loose.
But I wouldn't worry
about a fall of fruit
to bruising:
the magic that would make
the move
would catch the fruit
half-way
or turn the bruise
to gold.

ONE OF THE BOYS

Wanting to lie down on a bed
to read a book,
I am drawn not to the usual
marriage-bed but to the
lower bunk in my sons' room.

I lie down where Austin lies
each night, a seven-year-old
starting fresh, who has not unlearned
weeping at hurt, nor unlearned
the wild gesture that is like
the flash of an animal
escaping into the woods.

This is the male room,
where the mail of my life
has been piling up, unopened, for years.
I want to read it now
as I bask here in the exclusion
of all wives, mothers, daughters, even
lovers, even
the very best of witches.

A week ago I shared the room
of our car with my wife
as she drove us for the first time
to a marriage counselor. How far apart
two people in a car can be!
A glassy cave, and two
prototypes of the human
staring straight ahead

at the centuries-long task
of learning how to speak.
I wept then to think of Emmett,
whose dreams each night
are clouds moving like prophecies
across Austin's sky.

Now I fly in this lower bunk
into the future, the pilot
not to be seen
but believed, and felt
all around me in the form
of a magic circle,
a space the wizard carries
at all times inside him,
its power the source of any feat,
including the amazing
dissolution of walls between rooms.

FEBRUARY 14, 1980

The children pass phrases around
in a circle, whispering,
to see how they grow
into nonsense.

Yes becomes no.
McGillicuddy becomes
my pants are muddy.
Laughter accompanies

the worst mistakes of ear
and tongue. They are so young
to get so much so very wrong.
Are you listening now? And am

I speaking? Let tongue go inside
ear to fish around to make
it sure. Wife, the words
are coming fast, I strain, you

strain to catch a mere
three syllables with all
original intent intact.
Valentine. I love you.

The children roar again.
Boston beans are apple skins.
Dr. Seuss is termite juice.
Why is it if the sounds were true

from mouth to mouth
the game would all be lost?
Be mine, someone thinks
to say when his turn

comes round to make
a sacrifice to the spirit
of fun. He thinks again,
then says it anyway.

FROST WARNINGS

Tonight, a frost, perhaps,
so we lay sheets,
old ripped ones,
on the tomato plants

and a thin blanket long
the children's plaything,
plus any scraps we can find
big enough to drape a vine.

What a sagging
guardianship!
In the moonlight it looks
like a convention of ghosts

wornout and collapsed
from too much revelry
or worry. Who'd trust these
to fight a freeze?

Yet it is by
such measures
we daily
go,

it is the romance
of the tatterdemalion
that flies above our love
like a flag:

our comic jalopy
runs past credulity
and our old house sinks
like lovers into bed.

So we'll sleep well tonight,
giving, foolishly or not,
the care of the garden
to what is in decline,

as if, because of fall,
we choose the mortal.

THE LAST STRAW

One minute the camel was standing there,
   then it was not. I said it was her
straw that did it, she said it was mine.
   The fact is, if any one
of all those previous straws had been withheld,
   the camel would not now be dead.
So who can assign responsibility? Better
   just to say the spine by nature
was defective. I still hear its crack
   and shudder. I've heard jokes
about the sound, and I've laughed, because
   they were funny, but unless
you know the experience, you laugh too easily.
   The camel, as camels go, was a beauty,
less scruffy than most, and we had even begun to admire
   the hump. It was like a tower
inside which someone noble waits for rescue.
   If that someone flew
out when the camel fell in a heap before us,
   I didn't notice.
The mystery to me is why we did it,
   pile straw like that.
Maybe we thought camels needed a burden,
   to develop character, or that one
straw plus one straw plus one straw et cetera
   added up to a good way
to pass the time, our little game. More than
   likely, we did it for no reason
at all, a reflex, a gesture as of the arm
   of a sleeper. What could be the harm,
we must have thought, each piece was so light.
   It's true that now we can see straight

ahead, whereas before we always had to peer
   around, over, or under
that domesticated mass God designed
   not to sink in sand.
Still, I had begun to see patterns, a map
   even, on that skin, when I got up
close enough, though I hadn't figured out where
   North was. And I'll always remember
a look the camel gave me once: those great
   dark eyes wouldn't let
me go until I had translated them into
   this: "I am the master, you
are the beast I prepare for desert-
   duty." I was hurt
into a kind of joy. She, who put the straws
   on with me, no doubt has
a different camel-story to tell than mine.
   Every day now I see it shine
ahead of me, an oasis of witness,
   the sum of her days,
and watch it, as I approach, disappear
   into the burning air.

QUICKSONG

To do it less hungrily
To know nothing of Thief
To lie back and do it
(Late, soon, what matter?)
Under sun-round and moon

Under the spell of the garden, the air
Fruited thick, to pick
This or that, here or there
Always lips and a lover
Slower than bough-time can tell

To ease through the day
Vast passage with room
For us both and who we would be
Vistas open and opening wider—
Sight, and a beautiful yawn

To do it less hungrily
The table abundant
And still, never pressing
Upon us, the taking a choice
And forever to choose

And yes again yes
Every minute less
Hungrily
Hungrily
Quick one more kiss

WHERE WE WERE

It was a shadow scene.
Horses there would bolt
In the dim forest-flicker,
The limbs the wind took
Waved as if in lieu of words
That would not come to tell
The ways of half-light.
In that place wholly
Given, wholly unearned,
Nothing was either this or that,
We lived there in a kind of beauty
That was frightening, the spires of trees
Rose up to be swords in our eyes,
And low creatures moving
Dizzied us, who felt the needled
Floor go undulant.

Great crossings lived there,
Of light and dark, of earth
And projectiles from the earth,
Ascending things, that seemed
To want to go away.
We were caught at the crossing.

And when the trees would open,
The mass of the trees part as if
To let something through, nothing came through
Except everything beyond

The veil the rent trees were,
And I think it was enough for us.
No one complained, though our bodies
Made a music flecked with discord.
(How fine the discord flecked us,
A decoration for aristocrats!)

It was a place to walk, it was a place,
And we walked, birds fell at our feet,
Inexplicable manna,
The signs flew between trees
And shook the branches.
We trembled like the branches.
I held on to you, and you—
I think you flew between the trees,
My sign.

You could not call it wandering, what we did,
I think it was the place
That wandered in us,
We seemed so large.

IV / THE PRESENCE OF PRESENCE

LEVITATION

*A child watching a magician perform levitation
misses the point if he simply accepts miracles
and thinks the lady is actually floating through
the air.*—Judson Jerome

Wrong. She is floating.
And because she is floating
I can float, too.
And do.
Even now I am writing this poem
with both feet off the ground.
When I enter a room, inches
above the carpet, my wife and children
pass their hands around my body.
They discover no trickery.
I rise even higher.
I tell them, This is the height
from which I love you.
This is a miracle.
Or I approach friends
and sail over their heads
at the level of telephone poles,
floating like a moon
my dog howls at.
But whatever the high place,
I am holding the hand of the magician's
assistant. We are secret lovers.
I rise to her spangled costume
and lie against her, pillowed on the disbelief
of everyone who knows me.
I have fallen in love with her faith

in air. When I embrace her
and love her,
she whispers,
You have nothing to rely on.
Go higher,
higher.

THE BLIZZARD

He was a visitor, from the South,
and stuck at the farmhouse like the rest of us.
We'd told him, Don't go out there,
you think you know what it is and what it can do
but you don't,
but he insisted on going for a walk.
Now he was back inside, a snowman there before us,
and as he melted and shed his stiff clothing, he spoke.

"God is a blizzard, I know it now. That's the simple truth.
He's out there for anyone who wants to meet him.
And he's beautiful in his fierce way.
I mean it is a mask he wears, and hides behind,
but that we know him by the mask.
I'm going to move up here and never leave.
If it's good enough for God it's good enough for me.
Yes, you needn't say it,
I know people are getting lost out there in that,
but that's my point. It is something for our
selves to get lost in.
Oh, you look at me funny and I don't blame you.
But let me tell you, out there
there is a whiteness that is more than white.
As a child I was told black is the absence of all color
and white is the presence of all color,
color waiting to be broken up
into rainbow-revelation,
but now I say white is the presence
of Presence,
of what is and what wants you to come in to it and be, too.

"No, don't worry,
I'm not going back and never returning.

I'll have that drink of Scotch:
that's enough being for me at the moment;
I am no saint, though I would like to be.
But I swear by all that is cold,
by all that loves with white intensity,
that this is now my land,
that I will set up house here
and raise a storm of children
who will love storms
and what they are,
and that when I die here
it will be a kind of going blind in the snow,
a going blind from having seen too much."

We told him we had lived here all our lives
and there was nothing new he could tell us,
but that he was welcome, if he chose to stay.

PRAISEFUL MOUTHS

The dogs are barking at the carolers.
The dogs were sleeping till the songs began.
No sooner hark the herald than the fur
Rises along the neck, the back, the tail
Goes rigid. The Christ Child had no pet dog
But hung like a dog himself on the cross
Where no one sang to him except his father,
Whom the son couldn't hear. The dogs hear
The carolers, who hang notes in the sky
Like moons that craze the eye. They tramp the snow,
The moons do, the white musical targets
That bring peace to this bundled town tonight
By waking the dogs. Glory to the cold
Winds that keep the collars high. There shall be
Hot cider at the end, and murder, love,
Too, is a voice in the untrained choir,
With something to spike it all for those who
Take their winters seriously.
                              In go
The nails, in time to these amateurs,
Amo, amas, amat, who breathe smoke
With every praiseful mouth. There must be fire
Somewhere they will return, or discover
Walking with them, to set under the dogs
Who'll howl like gods choke-collared high in trees.
Adeste Fideles. It Came Upon
Them while they were sleeping, a dream to stir

The loins stars would someday shoot from, one
Star to lead them, down the street, past
The doghouses, into the rooms prepared
For company, the candles and cut glass
Cooperating to warm the singers
Stroking their fur, remembering that star.

THE RUNNER

How strange, he thought, that I should think myself
in training to meet death. That I prepare
my body for him. He thought that. As he ran.
He was thin. And getting thinner. The bones
that once were buried, happily, in flesh
were surfacing. Coming forward to meet
the eye. Or slowly developing like
a picture in a darkroom or the features
of a darkened room to a would-be sleeper.
The flesh was all a lie. The bones were true
and now were rising as he ran. To their
rightful place, in air. Like a word, a white
word, held back, so that no one heard
the light reflecting from it for so long
it dazzled now in taking on the day.
One had to learn to listen. He had to.
The ear could make out only, Bones, bones, bones.
The volume slow increasing. Gradual wave.
And no translation. Who spoke them, anyway?
Or it, the word they were. His feet, in time,
knew something. But they only beat the earth,
nor gave up what could carry him. That is,
as he carried the bones. So he carried
himself, like a gift. He was unwrapping
himself. As if the one the gift was meant
for were already here, were running, too.
The two of them. The one he'd come to meet
beside him. That shadow, scything the flowers
and leaving them intact.
                              How strange, he thought,
to glitter in the sun like this, the sweat
a wide and welcome riverrun, but yet

to be a sacrifice, a calf, a chastened
calf of only fat enough to be a
margin, line, between two worlds, the less
the more the traffic there, negotiation,
at that border infinite measures guard.
He thought that. As he ran. As he measured
off the miles. As his health and death
off-rhymed surprisingly on this country road,
a distinction lost in vapor like smoke
from a fire. The sun was burning itself up.
The sun ran its marathon. It ran through
pain. A pro. Or, better, amateur.
Amo, amas, amat. A lover. And he
had come to rendezvous. He thought that, too.

ONE OF THE SHADOWS

Two plus two equals five,
he said, and was right,
though it took us years
to find out.

We wanted corners, right angles,
the shadows clean across our lives,
but he said the shadows
entered our lives.
And he was right again.
He was one of the shadows.

Everywhere we looked, inside,
there he was, and his kind,
his cousins, his kind cousins,
all helping us against our wills
to a knowledge of numbers
that don't add up, their failure
a success of spirit.

One plus one plus one
equals nothing you can name
though three
has all the authority
and some people like that at every
meal, and in-between. They fatten.
Say, heads of state. He starved
and got so thin
he grew a crown
of crowns that left him
too heavy to lift.

Now we die to diet everything
away to put it on again
and have it, first time, fit.
At a feast. A feast
of wrong answers. This is one.
And the silence—that's another one.
But better. Because wronger.

PROOFREADING

There is no way to know
you have them all.
Who is going to say
there is no snake in the grass
just because you can't see it?
So you mow down the grass—
so what does that prove?
It proves that now there's a clearing
surrounded by grass. The grass goes on
and on. Love the grass
and what is
or is not in it.

If you're proofing your life,
you're weeding while reading.
Is it clean now? Remember
the Navajo weaver left a flaw
in the pattern, a loose thread, a tongue
to tickle the air, arouse it, so the god
of the air and all else would not be offended
by presumptuous perfection. Uppity.
Fire for the gods;
for men, typos.

There *is*
a snake in the grass
and his name is Desire.
Gold diamonds ride in file
his back, nor defile
him or his seat
of honor, our hearts,
heartland, grassland,
great plains like a sentence

stretching from here to there,
brushfires like commas
burning themselves up,
old buildings collapsing
like an object into its predicate,
a kiss into a gesture
of betrayal, a coming
that is a going.

Someone somewhere
has his fingers in the tray of type.
Praise him, curse him,
but let the curse appear as
course, a way,
and the praise as
praise, the mistake in the manuscript
that gets repeated in the final product,
book, breath,
and thereby, Proofreader,
becomes correct.

THE SLEEP

It is an answer, a going-into.
The soft helmet slowly eases over the head.
The limbs begin to believe in their gravity,
The dark age of faith begins, a god below
Draws down the body, he wants it
And we are flattered.
We are going to the level of water.
(Don't hold on. Drop fair, drop fair.)
This is fine seepage, we think,
Seepage raveling to a river
To set ourselves upon. So
What is the price of dark water?
Where is the weight going?
The body powers the vaguest of shapes,
Pilot-boat, the falls collapse
And collapse upon themselves. We hear them
In time and imitate them.
We would turn to water that has lost
Its floor, water surprisingly
In space and beading,
A glittering disintegration.
                        Now, what was a bed
Rocks just perceptibly, this is a cradle
In search of a captain, the bone-cargo
Settles, the medium
Washes up over and across and fills
The spaces we have been keeping empty just for this,
The palpable black herein
Barbarian, riding us down.
                        There will be a level
We come to, will we know it?
A flat place with, look, a light.

It is a guess as our loins give way.
Already we are forgetting
Where we were
And left from, the human
Faces like sunglare hurting our eyes.
Did we even wave goodbye? Yet could there
Possibly be someone here now,
That this going down
Not be so sole, and sore,
A cup, a cupped hand, a basket,
These forms of containment
Forms of Person
Where, when we're water, we're caught?
Listen. It is the sound of ourselves,
This passage: a breath.
We are almost not here.
If we break up this softly,
We must be incomparably lovely.

In memoriam, A. S., 1928–1974

THE WAY IT HAPPENS

So you trust like the birds
in God's goodness.
You refuse to calculate.
You go naked.
This lasts years.
You wander.
You are never satisfied.
That is the point.
Again you renew your trust.
Soon you begin
to peck at the ground.
You do not notice this.
You only know
you savor small grain.
Then you learn to make
a new sound.
This gives you pleasure.
You think nothing of it.
Next you develop nubs
at your side that grow
and feather.
You use these
to tuck in your head.
You believe that is not strange.
Finally, for no good reason,
you beat them.
You begin to fly.
By now you are not thinking
at all
of what you are doing.

PUTTING YOUR BODY TO SLEEP

Feet, for awhile now
be content to leave the good company of stones.

And Legs, don't worry so. It is mere foolish poetry
to think of yourselves as fallen trees.

Loins, I know how concerned you are
about your treasure. But believe me,
there are no thieves or murderers in sleep,
only rich, anonymous benefactors.

Chest, you lucky one. You alone need not be still.
Imagine—rising and falling all night like a sea.
And there will come to you
the strange sailors in swift ships
who follow the dark.

Now you, Arms. Lie still.
Remember the dreams in which,
disembodied and luminous,
you swing out like batons
past the farthest stars.
With luck, tonight . . .

Yes, Neck, I admit it: standing, you are a lovely tower.
But on your side, blown down, you are the tower
from which a prisoner has escaped. Think of him
running wildly over the countryside.

And Head. You pride yourself on wakefulness. That is good.
But in the dark there is someone I want you to meet.

About the Author

Philip Dacey teaches at Southwest State University in Minnesota. He is the author of *"How I Escaped from the Labyrinth" and Other Poems* and numerous chapbooks.

The Johns Hopkins University Press

*This book was composed in IBM Aldine Roman text
and display type by Horne Associates from a design
by Susan Bishop. It was printed and bound
by The Maple Press Company.*

G32667

PS3554
A23B6   Dacey, Philip.
               The boy under the bed. $10.95

5 3/00

12/99 ²